REVERSALS

Reversals

By Anne Stevenson

WESLEYAN UNIVERSITY PRESS

Middletown, Connecticut

#16195

Acknowledgement is gratefully made to the following periodicals, in the pages of which some of these poems were first published: *Analecta, Encounter, Generation, The Massachusetts Review, Michigan Quarterly Review,* and *Open Places.* Several of these poems were included in the book *Living in America,* published at the University of Michigan under the auspices of *Generation.*

Library of Congress catalog card number: 73–82545

Manufactured in the United States of America

First edition

For my family

CONTENTS

I

II

III

REVERSALS

Birth.
Impossible to imagine
not knowing how to expect.

Childbirth.
Impossible to imagine
years of the tall son.

Death.
Impossible to imagine,
exactly, exactly.

I

Among others it is the same. It is repeated.
A box not solid but with apertures
showing it to be, to the eye, hollow,
a container for light or noise,
not necessarily in three dimensions.

It might be the third in a series of mirrors,
It might be the real thing.

Whatever it is, it's clear it has claims on me.
Its surface establishes itself
outside and around me,
drawing me through or into
what I take to be my proper dominion.

These keys are my keys, this door my door.
The interior is entirely familiar.

At the same time, nowhere is my choice
evident as a force for arrangement.
What meaning has this long white chain
of machinery, even as teeth,
extended, or painted, to the point of its disappearance?

It waits in the silence of concealed energy.
It grins with the jaws of a piano.

Again, these interminable stairs, bristling with children.
"Mother, mother," they wail. They bleat with desire.
They quarrel and hold up their wounds to be kissed.
And yet when I bend to them
It is like kissing a photograph.

I taste chemicals.
My lips meet unexpectedly a flatness.

And here there are vases and reflections of vases
on the tables; and gardens,
and reflections in the windows of the gardens,
delphiniums and poppies, veins and arteries.
They compose an expensive anatomy.

The sunlight is apparently generated indoors.
The season is synthetic but permanent.

Look. I am free. I can go anywhere.
There is nowhere to go but on and on
into these soft contradictory perspectives,
corridors increasingly smoothed by carpets,
incandescent, metallic, immaculate, sweetened.

Nothing has happened. Nothing will happen.
There is neither an exit nor a reason for getting out.

What am I to do? Where am I to go?
The house has been entirely taken over by women.
To every corner they have brought their respectable destruction.
Listen and you can hear them bustling in my lost rooms,
sorting the dust into piles, embracing the furniture,
polishing, pummelling, scurrying, complaining,
pulling up the papers like weeds.
                                    Impossible to know
how not to enrage them. Their rules are exuded
inaudibly, vapors which congeal into speech
only when misunderstood. They are like music.
Every woman is an orchestra. Or an explorer,
a discoverer of uninhabitable moods. If they love me
it may be because I divest them of boredom.
I am useful as a conductor of superfluous energies.
But how through their wire-like waists and wrists
do their quick lusts slip, unresisted, into my lap?
Why do I allow them to litter my mind?

They moved in politely, not knowing who I was.
How pretty they were, flitting from mirror to mirror
in their gauze dresses. How delightful and thoughtful.
I should have known when they said they liked me
they liked tidying up messes, that they needed
rooms to have taste in, that little red pulses
beat I, I, I, under the most delicate skin.
Silence is what they're afraid of. They take precautions
always to move in a pack. Knowing also that loneliness
never attacks an argument, all the mothers
and sisters and daughters glare suspiciously
at each other over the tall generations, even when
they seem to be writing letters or playing the piano.

17

Not one of them forgets for a moment
I am able to escape. They make it my fault
that they have locked themselves up in my house.
They hate my free tempers and private indulgences.
But only the saint or the reprobate need not let
affection affect him. If I were a good man or
a bad man, I think I could make them leave. As it is,
they have made me believe in their attentions. I don't know
what I would want to replace them if they should go.

No time, no time,
and with so many in line to be
born or fed or made love to, there is no
excuse for staring at it, though it's spring again
and the leaves have come out looking
limp and wet like little green new born babies.

The girls have come out in their new bought dresses,
carefully, carefully. They know they're in danger.
Already there are couples crumpled under the chestnuts.
The houses crowd closer, listening to each other's radios.
Weeds have got into the window boxes. The washing hangs,
helpless. Children are lusting for ice cream.

It is my lot each May to be hot and pregnant,
a long way away from the years when I slept by myself—
the white bed by the dressing table, pious with cherry blossoms,
the flatteries and punishments of photographs and mirrors.
We walked home by starlight and he touched my breasts.
"Please, please!" Then I let him anyway. Cars
droned and flashed, sucking at the cow parsley. Later
there were teas and the engagement party. The wedding
in the rain. The hotel where I slept in the bathroom.
The night when he slept on the floor.

The ache of remembering, bitterer than a birth. Better
to lie still and let the babies run through me.
To let them possess me. They will spare me
spring after spring. Their hungers deliver me.
I grow fat as they devour me. I give them my sleep
and they absolve me from waking. Who can accuse me?
I am beyond blame.

This wet black soil has power beyond itself,
is capable of excrescence
beyond its power to imagine.
How easy it is for it to bear children.
How quick it is. A whole colony of flesh and pimples
adolescent in a night.

Don't touch them, they're evil. Squatters.
Members of an underprivileged sex.
No hands, no eyes, no bones,
just identical instruments of copulation.
If they grow to this size masturbating in darkness,
what will they do in the sun?

By nightfall they'll be bigger than the house.
Hairless, unable to support themselves, their big tips
will sway up over the rooftop,
thrust blindly into the rose bed where,
late, ripened secretly through the summer,
that red, red rose helplessly unseals her petals.

THE MOTHER

Of course I love them, they are my children.
That is my daughter and this my son.
And this is my life I give them to please them.
It has never been used. Keep it safe. Pass it on.

Don't think

that I don't know
that as you talk to me
the hand of your mind
is inconspicuously
taking off my stocking,
moving in resourceful blindness
up along my thigh.

Don't think
that I don't know
that you know
everything I say
is a garment.

AUBADE

Intervention of chairs at midnight.
The wall's approach, the quirkish ambivalence
of photographs, today in daylight,
mere pieces of balance. My brown dress,
tossed, messed, upheld by the floor.
Rags of ordinary washed light
draped as to dry on the brown furniture.
And the big bed reposed, utterly white,
that ached our darkness, rocked our weight.

LOVE POEM

You I embrace,
each eye my face,
hold me now
in my first darkness.
Let me stray through you
to the soft shock
of my beginning.
Stay and be witness
to this fluid rock
cooling and stiffening
in repeated rains.
Also to the sloth of hills building,
to the gathering of mountains.

As in my spirit he was conceived,
so of my body he is alone.
I am his clay, God's love made earth.
Old man, it was never Abraham's seed
swelled the globe of my virgin womb
and hung a new star over Nazareth!

When we loved
it was as if we created each other.
As if in my body two zeros,
two embryos
curved in the well of my sex.

But then you detached yourself,
you receded, transposed into pure sound—
a bell sharpening itself on its distance,
a blade honing itself to tremulous thinness—
while the mirror held me dumbly—my woman's face,
my body like a globe
nourishing its stray curl of flesh,
my huge breasts and body bound,
bound to the shape of this world.

The spirit is too blunt an instrument
to have made this baby.
Nothing so unskillful as human passions
could have managed the intricate
exacting particulars: the tiny
blind bones with their manipulative tendons,
the knee and the knucklebones, the resilient
fine meshings of ganglia and vertebrae
in the chain of the difficult spine.

Observe the distinct eyelashes and sharp crescent
fingernails, the shell-like complexity
of the ear with its firm involutions
concentric in miniature to the minute
ossicles. Imagine the
infinitesimal capillaries, the flawless connections
of the lungs, the invisible neural filaments
through which the completed body
already answers to the brain.

Then name any passion or sentiment
possessed of the simplest accuracy.
No. No desire or affection could have done
with practice what habit
has done perfectly, indifferently,
through the body's ignorant precision.
It is left to the vagaries of the mind to invent
love and despair and anxiety
and their pain.

I thought you were my victory
though you cut me like a knife
when I brought you out of my body
into your life.

Tiny antagonist, gory,
blue as a bruise. The stains
of your cloud of glory
bled from my veins.

How can you dare, blind thing,
blank insect eyes?
You barb the air. You sting
with bladed cries

Snail!   Scary knot of desires!
Hungry snarl!   Small son.
Why do I have to love you?
How have you won?

Gull, ballast of its wings.
Word, mind's stone.
Child, love's flesh and bone.

In the unbelievable days
when death was coming and going
in his only city,
his mind lived apart in the country
where the chairs and dishes were asleep
in familiar positions,
where the geometric faces on the wallpaper
waited without change of expression,
where the book he had meant to come back to
lay open on a bedside table,
oblivious to the deepening snow,
absorbed in its one story.

Alive in the slippery moonlight
how easily you managed
to hold yourself upright
on your small heels.
You emerged from your image
on the smooth fields
as if held back from flight
by a hinge.

I used to find you
balanced on your visible ghost,
holding it down by a corner. The blind
stain crawled, fawning, about you.
Your body staked its shadow like a post.
Gone, you leave nothing behind—
not a bone to hold steady or true
your image which lives in my mind.

Mother, I have taken your boots,
your good black gloves, your coat
from the closet in the hall, your prettiest things.
But the way you disposed of your life gives me leave.
The way you gave it away.
Even as I pillage your bedroom,
make off with your expensive, wonderful books,
your voice streams after me, level with sensible urgency.
And near to the margin of tears as I used to be,
I do what you say.

There may be a moon.
Look at the masklike complexion of the roof,
recognizable but relieved of familiarity.
The street, too. How weakened, unstable.
Shadows have more substance than the walls
they lean from. Thick phosphorescence
gathers in the spaces between window
and black window. Something subtle, like a moon,
has been creeping under surfaces,
giving them queer powers of illumination.

In this centerless light
my life might really have happened.
It rises, showing its wounds, longing for
abrasive penances. It touches me with a mania for
stealing moonlight and transforming it into my own pain.
I can feel myself closing like an eye.
I'm unable to look at the moon
or at anything pitted and white that is up there
painted on the sky.

Clouds—plainsman's mountains—
islands—inlets—flushed archipelagos—
begin at the horizon's illusory conclusion,
build in the curved dusk
more than what is always imaginary,
less than what is sometimes accessible.
Can you observe them without recognition?

Are there no landscapes at your blurred edges
that change continually away from what they are?
that will not lie, solid, in your clenched eye?
Or is love, in its last metamorphosis, arable,
less than what was sometimes imaginary,
more than what was usually accessible,
full furrows harvested, a completed sky.

II

ENGLAND
For Peter Lucas

Without nostalgia who could love England?
Without a sentimental attachment to tolerance
Who could delight in this cramped corner country
In no quarter savage, where everything done well
Is touched with the melancholy of understanding?

No one leaves England enamored,
But England remembered invites an equivocal regret.
For what traveller or exile, mesmerized by the sun
Or released by spaciousness from habitual self-denial
Recalls without wistfulness its fine peculiarities
Or remembers with distaste its unique, vulnerable surfaces?

Summer, and the shine of white leaves against thunder.
Ploughland where the wind throws the black soil loose
And horses pull clumsily as though through surf
Or stand, hoofs clapped to the earth like bells,
Braced in their pastures between churches and seagulls.
England.   Cool and in bloom,
Where the light grows like grass out of the ground,
Where the sky begets colors on uneasy seasons
And the hills lie down patiently in the rain.

Nowhere as in England is severity cherished
For its own sake or loneliness so compatible
With the soul. Where wilderness is scarcer than gardens,
Bare land is less dangerous than a cage of chimneys,
And the torn man flies to the small desolations
Where the wind can persuade him of vanity
Without diminishing his human importance.

Who derives innocence from the rain, from the broken
Silences of sheep, from houses lonely in an acre
On the smudged margins of centuries
Can never be wholly the prisoner of himself,
Hero or victim of his closed, difficult story.

His tragedy, like the sun, is oblique, precarious.
It occurs like a mistake, a reason for embarrassment,
A blunder in the saving ritual of endurance,
And therefore is forgiven and absorbed at last
Into the soft sound of the rain.

Americans like England to live in her cameo,
A dignified profile attached to a past
Understood to belong to her, like the body of a bust.
The image to the native is battered but complete,
The cracked clay flaking, reluctantly sloughed away,
Inadequately renewed on her beautiful bones.

The stinginess of England. The proliferating ugliness.
The pale boys, harmful, dissatisfied, groping for comfort
In the sodium darkness of December evenings.
Wet roofs creeping for miles along wet bricks.
Lovers urgently propping each other on the endless
Identical pavements in the vacant light
Where the cars live, their pupilless eyes
Turned upward without envy or disapproval.

Someone must live in the stunted houses behind the stucco.
Someone must feed from the tiny sick shops.
Someone must love these babies.

Unbelievable
In the murk of her cottage, the eighty-year virgin
Fussing over bottles and cats. The uncharitable cold.
Light falling in squares from the frugal windows
Of public houses. Schoolgirls dragging in crocodile
Through the damp lanes behind the converted castle,
Querulous in the big wind. In the same wind
That gathers them, together with the pylons and steeples
And gas drums, with the domes and scaffoldings and
    graveyards
And the small kempt gardens by the railway, helplessly,
Recklessly, untidily into the temporary spring.

Anglers appear, umbrellas and transistors
In the paths by the silted canals. And Sunday couples,
Spread like wet clothes on the banks.
Day unobstrusively seep into the nights,
Days that drew the daffodil after the crocus
And lit the rose from the embers of the hyacinth,
Thrust nettle and thistle through the ribs of abandoned
    machinery
And green the thick trunks of elaborate beeches.
Then the hills fill with remarkable gold wheat.

September.   Already autumnal.
Lost days drift in shapes under the plane trees.
Leaves tangle in the gutters.
In Greenwich, in Kew, in Hampstead
The paths are dry, the ponds dazed with reflections.
Come with me.   Look.   The city
Nourished by its poisons, is beautiful in them.
A pearly contamination strokes the river
As the cranes ride or dissolve in it,
And the sun dissolves in the hub of its own explosion.

That there should still be this.
Though memory and anticipation choose
Their own images of what has been or could be,
The seconds strike and are gone.
The season is gone that was a long time coming.
The fulfillment is like bread,
And the cornfields lie naked in the burnt shires.

No, not an end. A semblance of ending.
The change is without pause, is perfectly circular,
And the hand that breaks it is the hand that draws.
But we must believe the blunt evidence of our senses
As any physicist the map of his calculations,
As any child the reasonable comfort of his mother
That the leaves are beautiful because they are dying,
That the trees are only falling asleep.

SIERRA NEVADA
For Margaret Elvin

Landscape without regrets whose weakest junipers
strangle and split granite, whose hard, clean light
is utterly without restraint, whose mountains can purify
and dazzle, and every minute excite us but
never can offer us commiseration, never can tell us
anything about ourselves except that we are dispensable . . .

The rocks and water.
The glimmering rocks and the hundreds
and hundreds of blue lakes ought to be mythical,
while the great trees, as soon as they die,
immediately become ghosts,
stalk upright among the living with awful composure.
But even these bones that the light has taken and twisted,
with their weird gesticulations and shadows that look
as if they had been carved out of dust, even these
have nothing to do with what we have done or not done.

Now, as we climb on the high bare slopes, we find
the most difficult earth supports and the most delicate flowers:
Gilia and harebells, kalmia and larkspur, everywhere
the lupin's tight blue spires
and fine-fingered handshaped leaves.
Daintiest of all, the low mariposa, lily of the mountain,
with its honey stained cup and no imperfect dimension.
Strangest and highest, purple and yellow mosses
drink from their own furry stems.

If we stand in the fierce but perfectly transparent wind
we can look down over the boulders, over the drifted scree
with its tattered collar of manzanita,
over the groves of hemlock,

the tip of each tree resembling an arm
extended to a drooping forefinger,
down, down, over the whole, dry, difficult
train of the ascent, down to the lake
with its narrow, swarming edges where the little white boats
are moving their oars like waterbugs.

Nothing but the wind makes noise.
The lake, transparent to its greeny brown floor,
is everywhere else bluer than the sky.
The boats hardly seem to touch its surface. Just as
this granite is something that does not really touch us,
although we stand on it and see the color of its flowers.
The wind is strong without knowing that it is wind.
The twisted tree that is not warning or supplicating
never considers that it is not wind.
We think that if we were to stay here for a long time,
lie here like wood on these waterless beaches,
we would forget our names, would remember that
what we first wanted had something to do with stones,
the sun, the thousand colors of water,
brilliances,   blues.

This addiction!
The ones who get drunk on it easily!
The romantic, sad-hearted,
expensive inhabitants
who have to believe there is no way out,
who tear at themselves and each other
under the drumbeats while everyone
dances   or weeps
or takes off clothes hopefully,
half sure that the quivering bedstead
can bring forth leaves,
that love, love, love
is the only green in the jungle.

They are already old when the fen makes them,
Faces without features,
Flesh with the mud
And the slatternly weather,
Green water pulled from the weirs.

Fine rain smudges their level years,
Is food for their cabbages,
Smoke for their fires,
Veils for their eyes.
They keep to themselves behind shrouded glass.

Through their small doors no strangers pass.
Their viscid souls
Spawn a dejection
Too flat for pity.
It is not even grief that takes their voices
And leaves them glazed and lost in their houses.

Crazy birds in the blues of the campanile
Circling in sunlight the rings of orange and amber
Terraces dropped like haloes over the houses.
Umbria. Hoods of goldfish scales. But under
the glory, shaggy dwellings with deep claws
Clinging to Paradise shaped like a wide wheel.
Christ enthroned at the hub with the glimmering Virgin.
And saints stiff with respect among musical angels.
At the dangerous edges, the praying throng of the saved
Crushed into places on the disk circling the stage,
Spun out over the waste where the damned writhe
In crazy circles and orange fires burn.

For bungalows,
For weeded parlors,
For trained souls pinched in the bud,
The window boxes apologise.

Amid highbred
Miniature kindnesses,
The spinster gardens
Make polite, inaudible remarks.

Yes, for the
UnEnglish tourist
Who lives without tea
In a terrific country,

Who cannot,
In England, sufficiently
Diminish himself,
The gardens

Are unnecessary
As ubiquitous. The wilted
Curtains, the cold
Mercenary bathrooms,

He thinks,
Would be cheaper without them.
The blossoming carpets
And the teacups

And the shelves of
Useless, ornamental porcelain

Affect, he considers,
The price of his dinner.

He swears
And departs for Madrid.
Later, in Chicago or Dallas,
Will he ever think gently

Of the ladies
Planted in pairs in
Identical houses? Of the
Jars of lilac-colored soap?

Of the mournful
Decanters full of perfume or
Disinfectant? Of the roses,
The desolate neatness? The controlled despair?

Looking down at the village,
in the wind, in the winter,
in Hertfordshire,
they saw that the chimneys were praying,
warming the small insides of the houses
as the smoke swept into the air.

Somewhere nowhere in Utah, a boy by the roadside,
gun in his hand, and the rare dumb hard tears flowing.
Beside him, the greyheaded man has let one arm slide
awkwardly over his shoulder, is talking and pointing
at whatever it is, dead, in the dust on the ground.

By the old parked Chevy, two women, talking and watching.
Their skirts flag forward. Bandannas twist with their hair.
Around them some sheep and a fence and the sagebrush burning
and burning with its blue flame. In the distance, where
the mountains are clouds, lighting, but no rain.

Arriving in North Carolina after midnight,
Watched by the sheet-white sockets of the town,
Listened to by whitemen propped against the street light,
She found the one hotel and took a room.
Its walls were green. The hard bed wore a scroll
Of painted roses where the pillows met.
The air-conditioner on the window-sill
Roared and roared as the moth-white faces
Of her lovers poured from the gilded pelmet
And disappeared in the jaws of the open suitcases.
"Wait!" she cried, but the windows were stuffed with
      newspapers,
Niggerblack headlines buckling and billowing in.
She rose, trampling furiously. The papers and lovers
Dissolved. Were her lovers dead?
In their place stood an old man, wart on his chin,
Bundle of yellow newspapers up to his knees.
"Our paper comes out once a week," he said,
And shuffled behind the counter with the keys.

III

Clasped in its rigid head of bone,
The sea tosses,
Sleepless with tides.

Woman without body to the one moon.
Woman without shape.
Unborn faces.

Time in conception done and undone,
Unknown losses
Made and unmade.

MORNING

You lie in sleep
as liquid lies in the spoon
and sounds trouble a surface
which trembles without breaking.
The images flow and reverse—

the whistler, the walker,
the man worrying his accelerator,
the parabola of motors
in which the milkman moves—

just so, daily,
dissolving chromatics
of the commonplace
absorbed by the listening eye—

just so, rarely,
the language, the salvage,
the poem
not made but discovered.

DREAMING OF IMMORTALITY IN A THATCHED HUT

(After the painting by Chin Ch'ang-t'ang)

Drowsing over his verses or drifting
Lazily through the sutras,
He blinked in the hazy August silence
Through which a blind stream bore on
And the locusts endlessly sawed, performing mistakes
And catching themselves up again like nervous musicians.

The soft rain dropped on the dust at nightfall,
Dawns poured revelations over the peaks
Until, as he slept, he could see it all—
The graceful ascent from the shelving eaves of the hut.
The ease of detachment. The flowing out of his sleeves.
The slow half sorrowful movement of regret
As he rose with the steadying mists about his knees,
Away from the rocks and the stunted, gripping pine
And the books stacked neatly out of the way of the rain.

With their transparent black veils
Sustained in the air like cobwebs,
Nuns—shadows—glide through the dead leaves
Whispering with the hems of their skirts.
Chains, hanging from their waists,
Are beads and crosses.
Their businesslike notebooks
Are filled with impeccable handwriting.
In their faces, small circles of lines and flesh
Revolve in a closed landscape.
It is forever that they bow their voices,
Confirm in hushed inflections
What is renounced, what is decided upon.

The line between land and water
Forms itself without thought.
The land ends where, on the river,
No one can walk
Though the deep, familiar
Path looks hard as silver,
Though land can be held there
Firm in precise inversion
As an eye holds rock.

Neither side of the river
Is a mountain and no mind
Hesitates, moving from one
Bank to the other,
To cross the line.
Solid boats grow
In the ploughed slime.
Ducks with their hungry beaks
Break the water.

There is no end to illusion.
Swans' necks, clusters of pale stems,
Wave in the air.
Their tuberous bodies
Flower momentarily.
The river is full of fungi.
The scabby trunk
Breathes a steamy darkness
From under the scum.

At night the land slips softly
Into the river in vague
Columns of light. And the line
Between land and water
Forms in the eye
Of any casual observer
Who crosses the line
Between himself and object
Ceaselessly, without thought.

IN MARCH

The snow melts
exposing what was
buried there all winter—
tricycles and
fire-engines and
all sizes of children
waiting in boots and
yellow mackintoshes
for the mud.

In this
country, with its
effortless water,
its sea swung effortlessly
from long ropes in the hills,
its sky changing as the weather
turns and clouds break
on the spokes of the sun,
our discontents screen thinly
what is easy and profitable.

What richness do we not have?
Look! Pigs hatch from apples.
Cows ooze like sacks.
Children can be picked whole as cabbages
from our orchards and haystacks.
Our only frustration, such a strange one—
that we are forbidden to visit
the people of that
country.

Oh, we have heard
how in that
country rain is sweat,
the fields empty, scant as a map's.
How there is plenitude of mouths only.
How corpses are crops and
murder more casual than sleep.
Which one of us covets
their starved babies and
cratered villages?

Yet somehow
because of them
we are not at ease with ourselves.
We are good people.
We work diligently.
We would like to make sacrifices.
Something that is
not quite pity
broods over our lakes and
sours our huge loaves.

It's too big to begin with.
There are too many windless gardens
walled to protect eccentric vegetation
from a crude climate.
Rare shoots, reared in glass until
old enough to reproduce themselves,
wholly preoccupy the gardeners
who deliberately find it difficult
to watch each other, having planted themselves
head downwards, spectacles
in danger of falling off over their thumbs.

Some beds bear nearly a thousand petunias.
Others labor to produce one rose.
Making sense of the landscape, marking distinctions,
neat paths criss-cross politely,
shaping mauve, indigo and orange hexagons,
composing triangles and circles
to make the terrain seem beautiful.

But to most of the inhabitants
these calculated arrangements are
not only beautiful but necessary.
What they cultivate protects, is protected from
the man-eating weeds of the wilderness,
roses of imaginary deserts,
watered by mirage, embellished
by brilliant illusory foliage, more real
for having neither name nor substance.

THE WATCHERS

It is wise of our enemy to rely upon the watchers.

Wired with a precision that makes nerves anachronisms,
controlled from tall skeletons of electromagnetic steel,
they are dangerous without risk to themselves.
They envisage no distinction.
They anticipate no destruction.
                    They are not alive.
Yet they have ears and eyes no
rustle escapes, no flicker misses.

They hover at a level above breathable air,
                    but are also near,
In our shoes and telephones.
In our pillows.   In our spoons.
Even when we say nothing,
what passes in our brains
is traced in encephalogram by their ticking.
We are aware of them when we make love.

And because they are unapproachable through anguish,
inaccessible to madness as to argument,
we are more afraid of them than of the great holocaust.
Yet hating and fearing them as we do,
it is curious how often we are exhilarated.
It is as if we had acquired new souls.
Have we forgotten how to be bored?
Are we delivered forever from loneliness?
Are we worthy, we wonder, of the marvel of such attention?

On the face of it, smooth. The blond silences.
Mouths out for ice cream or love in the park.
Women's flat eyes and wispy indulgences.
Their ordinary husbands. Their ordinary lives.
Are they making them up as they lie in the dark?

Or are the real dreamers the thin excitables who
Lie awake listening, listening in bed
And think they can hear the world being drilled through?
They think it resembles a mummified head,
The brain sucked dry through the sockets;
Or an old dry garrulous balding head,
Kept alive by experiment.   Useless.

"I have been long.
The long war is over.
Love, I am back.
I was lucky, brave.
Here, dark in the dark,
Sleep drops like a shudder.
That step is my heart
In its lonely cave."

"You have been long,
And your steps, your slow steps,
Are these tracks on my hands
Which will never warm.
And these in my bones,
Through my bony hips,
This chest with its bones
You could play with your thumb."

HERAKLES AND THE OLD ONE
To A. C. Graham

Alive, malleable, evasive of cold shape,
Hunted, held thrashing, evolving in my grasp,
Finned, amphibious, feathered, limbed at last
Through the coal-engendering chaos. You do not escape.
The dazzlement of indéfinance corruscates, promising nothing.
Even in this plasmic brightness, pulsing with noises,
You are alive still, melting at my fingertips.
Have you instead caught me? Is it I who am changing?

You harden in spite of yourself, urging me to strength.
Confess. You belong to me. You breathe with my breath.
Terrible in your aspects, not one will I abandon—
Amoeba, archaeopteryx, nematode, dolphin,
Cobra and sparrow-hawk, sparrow and gap-toothed rat.
Monster, make me your victim.   Equip me with fleetness.
Woman, make me your embryo.   Release me into childhood.
Youth, make me your harlot.   Hold me to your lips.

All that you demand I become through grace of strength.
Strength.   Strength.   It shall discover you,
No hoary sea-god barnacled with legends,
No father of slime, herding your daughters,
But as pure element, clean as blown dust.
I shall be purged of strength, then, restored to you
Immaculate.   As one is delivered immaculate
To the embrace of the sun or to a long sleep.

THE END OF IT

Let darkness come down
Like sleep to our murderous star.
The wound is clean.
A cold wind bathes the scar.
What we have done
Divides us from what we are.
But the pain is over,
The last nerve dead,
And dark takes the town
As sleep the lover,
As sleep the child in its bed.

Distinguished contemporary poetry in cloth and paperback editions

ALAN ANSEN: *Disorderly Houses* (1961)

JOHN ASHBERY: *The Tennis Court Oath* (1962)

ROBERT BAGG: *Madonna of the Cello* (1961)

MICHAEL BENEDIKT: *The Body* (1968)

ROBERT BLY: *Silence in the Snowy Fields* (1962)

GRAY BURR: *A Choice of Attitudes* (1969)

TURNER CASSITY: *Watchboy, What of the Night?* (1966)

TRAM COMBS: *saint thomas. poems.* (1965)

DONALD DAVIE: *Events and Wisdoms* (1965); *New and Selected Poems* (1961)

JAMES DICKEY: *Buckdancer's Choice* (1965) [National Book Award in Poetry, 1966]; *Drowning With Others* (1962); *Helmets* (1964)

DAVID FERRY: *On the Way to the Island* (1960)

ROBERT FRANCIS: *The Orb Weaver* (1960)

JOHN HAINES: *Winter News* (1966)

EDWIN HONIG: *Spring Journal: Poems* (1968)

RICHARD HOWARD: *The Damages* (1967); *Quantities* (1962)

BARBARA HOWES: *Light and Dark* (1959)

DAVID IGNATOW: *Figures of the Human* (1964); *Rescue the Dead* (1968); *Say Pardon* (1961)

DONALD JUSTICE: *Night Light* (1967); *The Summer Anniversaries* (1960) [A Lamont Poetry Selection]

CHESTER KALLMAN: *Absent and Present* (1963)

PHILIP LEVINE: *Not This Pig* (1968)

LOU LIPSITZ: *Cold Water* (1967)

JOSEPHINE MILES: *Kinds of Affection* (1967)

VASSAR MILLER: *My Bones Being Wiser* (1963); *Onions and Roses* (1968); *Wage War on Silence* (1960)

W. R. MOSES: *Identities* (1965)

LEONARD NATHAN: *The Day the Perfect Speakers Left* (1969)

DONALD PETERSEN: *The Spectral Boy* (1964)

MARGE PIERCY: *Breaking Camp* (1968); *Hard Loving* (1969)

HYAM PLUTZIK: *Apples from Shinar* (1959)

VERN RUTSALA: *The Window* (1964)

HARVEY SHAPIRO: *Battle Report* (1966)

JON SILKIN: *Poems New and Selected* (1966)

LOUIS SIMPSON: *At the End of the Open Road* (1963) [Pulitzer Prize in Poetry, 1964]; *A Dream of Governors* (1959)

ANNE STEVENSON: *Reversals* (1969)

RICHARD TILLINGHAST: *Sleep Watch* (1969)

JAMES WRIGHT: *The Branch Will Not Break* (1963); *Saint Judas* (1959); *Shall We Gather at the River* (1968)